SHIRE NATURE

Butterflies
of the British Isles:

THE PIERIDAE

MICHAEL EASTERBROOK

CONTENTS

Cover: *Male orange-tip.*

Series editor: Jim Flegg.

Copyright © 1989 by Michael Easterbrook. First published 1989.
Number 50 in the Shire Natural History series. ISBN 0 7478 0031 6.

Printed in Great Britain by C. I. Thomas & Sons (Haverfordwest) Ltd, Press Buildings, Merlins Bridge, Haverfordwest, Dyfed

Introduction

Members of the family Pieridae are predominantly white, yellow or orange butterflies. The colours are mainly due to pigments, those of the white butterflies being formed from waste products of the insects' metabolism. Pierids occur in most parts of the world, with 41 species in Europe of which six species are resident in the British Isles. In addition, three species of clouded yellow migrate to Britain and breed in some years.

The best known of the British Pierids are the notorious 'cabbage whites', which are very important pests of cultivated brassicas. Two species are involved, the small white and the large white. The small white was introduced accidentally into North America about 1860 and to New Zealand and Australia in the 1930s and became an important pest in those countries also. Worldwide crop losses from these two species have been estimated at many millions of pounds annually.

NAMES AND FOLKLORE

The word butterfly is probably derived from the 'butter-coloured fly' seen early in the year — the brimstone, which is a Pierid. The brimstone is itself named after its sulphur-yellow colour. That other harbinger of spring now called the orange-tip was once known by the rather lovely and apposite name 'lady of the woods'. The Bath white, a rare summer visitor to Britain, was so named because a lady from Bath, Avon, executed a piece of needlework in which this butterfly was depicted.

The cabbage whites have always been less popular than other species and were often named after groups of locally unpopular people. Thus in Lincolnshire they were called Frenchmen, and in Westmorland Papishes (after Roman Catholics) and were hunted by gangs of boys on Oak Apple Day (May 29th). In many other parts of Britain bounties were paid for whites to encourage their destruction. The Latin name of their genus (*Pieris*), however, derives from the nine muses of Greek mythology, who inspired the arts and learning.

MIGRATION

Several species in the family Pieridae undertake large-scale migrations, including the small and large whites and the clouded yellows. In the British Isles there is usually a northerly migration of large whites in spring and summer and a return southerly movement in the autumn. The numbers involved can be very large, particularly in other parts of Europe. The width of a migrating mass of butterflies has been estimated at 4 km (2½ miles) in some cases. During one migration in Germany it was estimated that two million butterflies flew past a 100 metre transect each hour, the equivalent of 300 to 400 million individuals over the duration of the flight! Such migrations have been likened to snowstorms and have also been observed over the sea. It is not known how far most butterflies move, but one individual marked in Germany was recaptured 95 km (60 miles) away.

Large whites come to the British Isles in two waves, the first usually in late May and early June and the second in late July and early August. It is not certain from what parts of Europe they originate, though many are probably from southern Scandinavia and the Baltic Islands.

The various species of clouded yellows are well-known migrants. Numbers reaching the British Isles vary a great deal from year to year. For many years records of migrant butterflies throughout Britain have been collated by R. Bretherton and M. Chalmers-Hunt, and their records illustrate these variations. In 1983 over 13,000 clouded yellows were recorded, including some that were the offspring of earlier migrants. This was by far the highest annual total recorded since the phenomenal 'clouded yellow year' of 1947, when over 30,000 were seen. During most of the second half of the twentieth century numbers reaching Britain have been low, with less than ten recorded in 1963, 1972 and 1974. These large differences in numbers probably reflect variations in breeding success in continental Europe, the availability of foodplants there and variations in weather patterns.

NATURAL ENEMIES

Depredations by the whites would be

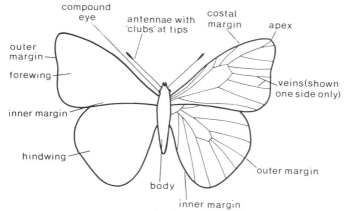

1. *Generalised diagram of the upper side of a butterfly.*

even greater were it not for the efforts of various natural enemies that attack them. One of the reasons that the small white became such a serious pest in the countries into which it was introduced was that it was able to multiply unchecked by many of the natural enemies that reduce its numbers in Europe. The most important of these are various species of parasitoids, tiny wasps only a few millimetres long. Foremost amongst them is a Braconid wasp called *Apanteles glomeratus* (figure 2), which lays its eggs in a caterpillar using its needle-like ovipositor. Over one hundred eggs are sometimes laid in a single caterpillar, usually when it is about half-grown. When the wasp larvae hatch they live and grow in the body of their victim, feeding on the blood and fat but avoiding the vital organs, until the caterpillar is ready to pupate. The fully fed wasp larvae finally emerge through the skin of the host and spin their yellow cocoons around the withered remains (figure 2). However, even the *Apanteles* larvae are not safe, as they may themselves be attacked by an even smaller wasp, a process known as hyperparasitism. *Apanteles* was taken from England and released in the United States of America to combat the introduced small white which was causing

2. *Caterpillar of large white, with mass of cocoons of the parasitic wasp Apanteles glomeratus. The grubs of the wasp have fed inside the caterpillar's body before leaving it to pupate. The body of the adult Apanteles glomeratus (right) is 2.5 mm long.*

3

serious damage to brassica crops.

Pierids are also attacked at various stages of their life-cycle by other parasites. Another wasp, called *Trichogramma*, is so minute that its larvae develop within the eggs of the butterfly. The chalcid wasp *Pteromalus puparum* lays its eggs in the newly formed chrysalises of white butterflies. When the small white became a serious pest in New Zealand after its accidental introduction there, parasitised pupae were taken there and the wasps that emerged were released. Since then the butterfly has been kept under control. Tachinid flies may also be important parasites in some years.

Caterpillars of Pierid butterflies are also attacked by various bacteria, fungi, protozoa and viruses. A granulosis virus, probably introduced by immigrant butterflies, was first seen infecting the caterpillars of white butterflies in Britain in 1955 and has caused high mortality since that time.

Various predators also feed on Pierids. Birds, particularly sparrows, are important predators of some species. Large white larvae are rejected by some birds, however, presumably because they are distasteful. They certainly have an unsavoury smell and can eject a defensive secretion from the mouth when disturbed. The caterpillars feed in groups and jerk their bodies when disturbed, which may deter would-be predators. Caterpillars are also attacked by ground beetles, hoverfly larvae, harvestmen and other general predators.

CHOICE OF EGG-LAYING SITES

One of the most fascinating aspects of Pierid ecology is the way in which the female butterflies choose plants on which to oviposit and there has been considerable research on this subject. Many Pierids do not lay eggs on any plant of their food species but show distinct preferences for particular plants. Small and large whites and orange-tips tend to lay eggs on those plants at the edges of a group. They also show a preference for the largest plants. In contrast, R. Dennis showed that green-veined white females actively selected small turnip plants in areas of low density.

Research by S. Courtney showed that orange-tip females are attracted by a range of size factors operating at different scales, such as larger dense patches of foodplant, taller plants, and larger and more numerous flowers. However, another factor comes into play, as orange-tips and large whites seem able to detect the presence of eggs of their species already present on a foodplant and will usually avoid laying more, thus avoiding increased competition for food.

At close quarters, recognition of the

3 (left). *Caterpillar of small white with pupa of a parasitic wasp, probably Microgaster sp. The larva of the wasp has fed inside the caterpillar and killed it.*

4 (right). *Chrysalis of orange-tip, attached to a stem by a thin girdle of silk.*

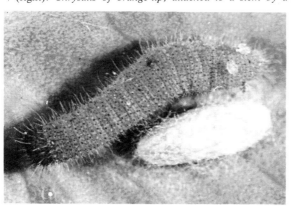
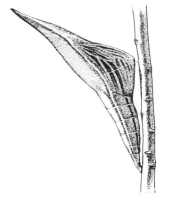

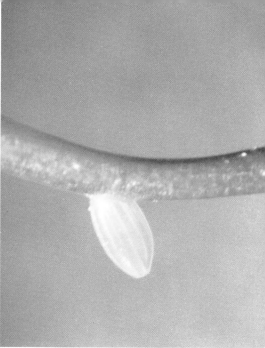

5 (above left). *Orange egg of orange-tip on flower stalk of garlic mustard.*

6 (above right). *Close-up of orange-tip egg.*

7 (below left). *Caterpillar of orange-tip on seed pods of garlic mustard.*

8 (below right). *Underside of orange-tip showing mottled pattern of yellow and black scales.*

foodplant by a female is the result of detecting plant odours and the chemical composition and texture of the leaf. The antennae of the butterfly can distinguish suitable plants and the tarsi (feet) can also detect chemicals present in the plant.

The whites

ORANGE-TIP, *Anthocharis cardamines*

The appearance of orange-tip butterflies in spring is always a welcome sight. The males, in particular, are very beautiful with vivid orange tips to the forewings (figure 9 and cover). The females do not have any orange coloration. They have grey-black tips to the forewings and a large black spot in the centre of the forewing upperside (figure 11) and so may be mistaken for small whites when in flight. However, this species is easily distinguished from other whites when the undersides of the hindwings are visible because in both sexes these have an attractive green marbling on the white background (figures 8 and 10). The green colour comes from a mixture of yellow and black scales. This patterning provides superb camouflage when the butterfly is at rest on vegetation. This species is fairly small, with a wingspan of 45 to 50 mm.

The eggs are laid on various crucifers, usually on the stalks of the flowers. The most commonly used foodplants are lady's smock (*Cardamine pratensis*) and garlic mustard (*Alliaria petiolata*), but others such as hedge mustard (*Sisymbrium officinale*), charlock (*Sinapis arvensis*), and watercress (*Nasturtium officinale*), may sometimes be used. In gardens honesty (*Lunaria annua*), dame's violet (*Hesperis matronalis*) and *Arabis albida* may be chosen. This range of foodplants enables orange-tips to breed in a wide range of habitats.

The bottle-shaped eggs are very pale green when first laid but soon turn orange (figures 5 and 6) and so, with practice, are relatively easy to find. Usually only one egg is laid on a flowerhead. The larvae are cannibals and, if several eggs are laid on a plant, the first to hatch will often destroy the other eggs or small

larvae, thus ensuring an adequate amount of food is available for its own development.

The caterpillars are pale orange with black hairs when young, becoming blue-green on the back and dark green underneath, with a white stripe along the sides. They are long and thin and very well camouflaged when sitting on the seed pods which provide their main source of food (figure 7). The caterpillars can be found in June and early July, after which they leave the foodplant to pupate among dense vegetation. The chrysalis is an attractive structure with a distinctive triangular shape, and is anchored by a fine loop of silk (figure 4). It is usually pale brown, though sometimes green.

Orange-tips usually appear in late April or May, with the males on the wing first. They can be seen until June or even early July. Since the 1970s this butterfly appears to have been extending its range into northern England and Scotland. This spread may have been facilitated by a series of cool Aprils which delayed emergence of butterflies in those regions until May. This month usually has much better weather than April, particularly in northern regions, and thus provides better conditions for the flight needed for egg-laying and to colonise new areas. The orange-tip has now reoccupied the areas it inhabited in the first half of the nineteenth century and has even exceeded them in some regions. In the latter part of the nineteenth century and the first half of the twentieth it disappeared from southern Scotland and much of the north of England. Happily, this trend is now being reversed, for example in the Newcastle upon Tyne area it reappeared in 1976 after an apparent absence of over one hundred years.

In southern England orange-tips occur along lanes, in meadows, woodland glades and marshy areas and along riverbanks. In northern Britain its distribution is less continuous, corresponding with a more restricted choice of suitable habitats, and it is mainly found along riverbanks.

Despite the success of this species in extending its range, on a local scale there has undoubtedly been a considerable decline in areas of intensive agriculture.

Here many hedgerows have been removed and damp meadows drained, in both cases removing foodplants in the process. Indiscriminate mowing and spraying of herbicides on roadside verges by local authorities also destroys many foodplants.

GREEN-VEINED WHITE, *Artogeia (Pieris) napi*

This butterfly is often mistaken for a small white and so is considered unwelcome in the garden. However, its larvae rarely feed on cultivated brassicas but rather are found on wild crucifers such as garlic and hedge mustards, lady's smock, watercress and, less often, on charlock and large and hairy bitter-cress (*Cardamine amara* and *C. hirsuta*). There are also records from other crucifers such as creeping yellowcress (*Rorippa sylvestris*).

The green-veined white can be distinguished from the small white by the grey-green outlining of the veins on the underside of the wings (figure 15), though these markings may be faint on second (summer) brood females. The veins on the upperside are also marked with grey, except on first (spring) brood males (figures 12 and 13). The upperside markings are stronger on summer brood adults (figure 14). The tips of the forewing have dark marks which extend further down the outer margin than on the small white. On the forewing upperside there are two black spots in the female, one in the male. The wingspan is very variable, often around 45 mm, but it can be as small as 25 mm.

The pale, bottle-shaped eggs are laid singly on the underside of the leaves of the foodplants. The caterpillars are dark green with yellow rings around the spiracles (breathing holes) (figure 16) and lack the yellow stripe found on the small white larva. They feed mainly on the leaves, thereby largely avoiding competition with orange-tip larvae, which utilise the same foodplants but eat the seed pods. The chrysalis is formed among dense vegetation and occurs in various colour forms, ranging from green to pale brown. The butterfly overwinters in this stage. Depending on latitude, altitude and the weather in any particular year, in Britain the green-veined white may have one, two, or even three generations of adults in a year. In the south there are usually two broods of adults which overlap, so that they may be seen at any time from late April to September, with the highest numbers usually seen in August. Occasionally there is a small third brood in late September. At high altitudes and in parts of Scotland there may only be a single brood, in June and July.

Green-veined whites occur in a variety of habitats, depending on which foodplant they are using: along hedgerows, verges and the edges of woods where hedge and garlic mustards and charlock grow; in damp meadows or marshes where lady's smock is plentiful; and along the edges of slow-flowing streams containing watercress. In northern England and Scotland they are usually associated with damp meadows or marshes and occur in isolated colonies, each with relatively small numbers of butterflies (up to forty) and often separated by several miles. Further south populations often occur in woodland or hedgerow habitats, where colonies are less discrete.

The green-veined white is one of the most common and widespread butterflies in the British Isles. There was a decline in numbers after the drought of 1976, but populations soon built up again. This species occurs over most of the British Isles, though it is absent from parts of the central and north-west Highlands of Scotland and the Shetland Isles.

SMALL WHITE, *Artogeia (Pieris) rapae*

This is the commonest butterfly in urban areas of Britain and second only to the meadow brown overall. It is most abundant in areas where cultivated brassicas are grown, as these are its main foodplants. The small white occurs over most of the British Isles, though it is absent or rare in the Outer Hebrides and Shetlands. Its range extends throughout Europe and Asia and, since its introduction, North America, Australia and New Zealand.

Small whites can be seen during most of the period from April to September or October, as they have two or even three generations per year. Numbers are usual-

9. *Male orange-tip.*

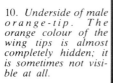

10. *Underside of male orange-tip. The orange colour of the wing tips is almost completely hidden; it is sometimes not visible at all.*

11. *Female orange-tip.*

12. *Green-veined white (spring brood).*

13. *Green-veined white (spring brood) with veins more heavily marked.*

14. *Green-veined white of the second (summer) brood. Note the darker, more extensive markings on the uppersides of the wings than on the spring brood.*

ly highest in the second generation, and there may be reinforcement of resident populations by migrants at this time. There are some differences in appearance of butterflies from the two broods as well as between sexes (figure 21). The markings at the tips of the forewings and the spots near the centre of the forewings are much fainter in the spring brood and may be completely absent in the male. The male usually has a single spot on the upperside of the forewing; the female has two merging spots below the centre of the forewing in addition to the single spot. Both sexes have attractive yellow undersides to the hindwings and yellow tips on the underside of the forewings (figure 18). The wingspan averages 48 mm.

The pale yellow, bottle-shaped eggs are laid on the undersides of leaves. Although laid singly, there may be several on one plant. Individuals have been recorded laying several hundred eggs. The caterpillars live solitarily and bore into the hearts of cabbages, so differing from those of the large white which feed gregariously on the outer leaves. When fully grown the small white larva is green sprinkled with black, and has a yellow line down the back and a line of yellow spots along each side (figure 17). The larval stage lasts about three weeks, after which the chrysalis is formed, sometimes on the plant but often on a fence or building. The colour can be adapted to that of the background, varying from pale brown through grey to green.

The caterpillars feed on cultivated brassicas such as cabbages, brussels sprouts and cauliflowers, also on garden nasturtiums and on wild crucifers such as hedge and garlic mustards, hoary cress (*Cardaria draba*) and wild mignonette (*Reseda lutea*). There is a tendency for most eggs to be laid on plants in sheltered situations.

LARGE WHITE, *Pieris brassicae*

This species looks similar to the small white but is usually larger, with a wingspan normally in the range of 60 to 70 mm. The other major distinguishing feature is that the dark tip to the forewing extends much further down the outer margin than on the small white, where it is confined to the extreme tip (figures 24

and 23). These tip markings are greyish in the spring brood but much blacker on summer butterflies. The female large white is larger than the male and has two large black spots on the forewing, visible on both sides of the wing, whereas in the male these spots are only present on the underside (figure 22). Much of the underside of both sexes is pale yellow, dusted with grey (figure 25).

Large whites may be seen from April or May until September or October, with a gap in July in some years. There are usually two generations of adults in a year in southern Britain, but in a warm summer there may be a partial third brood. In parts of northern Britain there may be only one generation per year. Populations usually peak in the second generation where this occurs, and numbers may be swelled by migrants from continental Europe.

The bright yellow, bottle-shaped, ribbed eggs are laid in groups, often of fifty to a hundred eggs, in several neat rows on leaves (figure 19) and can easily be spotted. They may be laid on either side of the leaf, the female being able to bend her abdomen around the margin of the leaf to attach them to the underside. The caterpillars feed in groups, exposed on the leaves of the foodplant (figure 20). They are able to behave with such impunity because they assimilate from the plant chemicals called mustard oil glycosides, which render them distasteful and toxic to predators. The markings of these caterpillars — yellow and black markings on a blue-green background — are a warning, advertising their unpalatability. As a result, many predators avoid the larvae, though some birds will take them. The bodies of the caterpillars also contain supercooling substances, a form of 'antifreeze', which enable them to withstand frosty conditions.

The larvae feed voraciously in groups and can soon reduce the leaves of a plant to a skeleton. After passing through five larval instars (stages), involving four moults, the caterpillar is ready to form a chrysalis, often walking considerable distances to find a suitable site. Typical places are under copings on walls, on fences and under windowsills. Earlier in the twentieth century, in years of very high numbers, some consternation was caused by the caterpillars invading houses in search of pupation sites. The chrysalis is green or yellow-green with black markings and short spines.

As well as attacking brassicas such as cabbages, brussels sprouts and cauliflowers, caterpillars will feed on nasturtiums and mignonettes. Over eighty foodplants have been recorded worldwide, mostly in the family *Cruciferae*, though also some *Tropaeolaceae*. Female butterflies are able to detect the odour of the volatile chemicals contained in these plants and are attracted to them for egg-laying.

Large whites are strong, fast fliers, with speeds in excess of 15 km/h (9 mph) recorded. They occur throughout Europe, in North Africa and in Asia Minor as far as the Himalayas, and have been recorded from virtually every part of the British Isles. Populations in Britain are regularly augmented by migrants from continental Europe. Large whites appear to be less numerous than in the past, when reports mentioned cabbage fields 'thick with whites' and migrations that appeared like snowstorms, blotting out the sun. The decline in numbers is probably due to a combination of factors, including more effective insecticides and the increasing prevalence of virus disease. There are certainly plenty left to trouble gardeners in most years.

WOOD WHITE, *Leptidea sinapis*

This fragile-looking butterfly is the smallest of the British whites, with a wingspan around 42 mm. Its flight is feeble in comparison with other Pierids. The butterfly always rests with wings closed, so that only the undersides are visible. The ground colour of these is yellowish-white, on which there are darker patches composed of grey-green scales (figure 27). The green tinge is particularly evident on Irish specimens. The males have black tips to the uppersides of the creamy-white forewings, whereas females have merely a dusting of grey scales in this position. The wings are more rounded and the body is much thinner than in other British whites.

Wood whites fly in May, June and July and there may be a second generation in August at southern sites in warm summers. Males emerge first in the spring and may be seen drinking at puddles or on mud. After mating, females search for the foodplants, mainly meadow vetchling (*Lathyrus pratensis*), bitter vetch (*L. montanus*), tufted vetch (*Vicia cracca*) and sometimes bird's-foot trefoil (*Lotus corniculatus*). The off-white, bottle-shaped eggs are laid on the undersides of the leaves of these plants, with a preference shown for those protruding above the surrounding vegetation in sunny, sheltered positions. The tubular-shaped caterpillars are pale green with a darker green stripe down the back and a yellow stripe along each side. They feed on the leaves of the foodplant, becoming fully grown in July when they form a green, angular chrysalis (figure 29) amongst dense vegetation. Winter is spent in the chrysalis stage.

As its name implies, the wood white is predominantly a woodland butterfly, at least in most of mainland Britain. In south Devon it occurs on the undercliffs of the coast, however, and in Ireland and in continental Europe it also occupies more open situations. This species is fairly common in Ireland but has always been extremely local in England and has become even more restricted in range during the last hundred years. It became extinct from most of its northern and eastern sites in the nineteenth century and was also lost from the New Forest and the Isle of Wight at this time. The present distribution is centred in three main areas — Hereford and Worcestershire, Northamptonshire and Oxfordshire, and on the Surrey-Sussex border. There are also scattered colonies throughout south-west England.

One of the main reasons for the decline in populations of wood whites is likely to have been the reduction in the area of woods managed by coppicing. This has led to the disappearance of the open areas and rides where the foodplants of this butterfly flourish. Research by M. Warren and colleagues at the Institute of Terrestrial Ecology has revealed some of the complex ecological requirements of this butterfly. It seems that the numbers of eggs laid do not depend solely on the abundance of the foodplant, but rather

15. *Underside of green-veined white (spring brood). Vein markings are fainter in summer butterflies.*

16. *Caterpillar of green-veined white.*

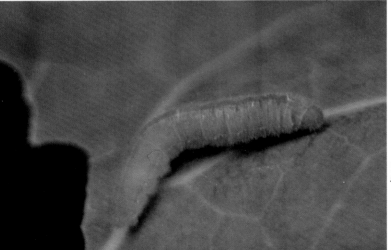

17. *Caterpillar of small white.*

18. *Underside of small white.*

19. *Clusters of eggs of large white on a cabbage leaf.*

20. *Caterpillars of large white.*

on its growth habit under differing shade conditions. In conditions of 20 to 50 per cent shade *Lathyrus* tends to project above the shrubby surrounding plants and it is on these taller foodplants that most eggs are laid, leading to successful colonies. Females appear to search for suitable oviposition sites in a range of shade conditions, but the number of eggs they lay depends on the frequency with which they encounter suitable foodplants. They do not seem to find the plants by sight, but instead they fly amongst vegetation, alighting frequently and testing the foliage with the antennae and front tarsi.

Wood whites appear to have poor powers of dispersal and so are slow to colonise new areas. However, since 1970 there has been some expansion of range and there are now believed to be over ninety colonies in England and Wales. Some of this increase is probably due to the increased area of young conifer plantations, which provide rides with foodplants and also flowers to provide the adults with nectar. However, as these plantations mature they become unsuitable as shading increases. Conservation of this species is, therefore, likely to depend on appropriate woodland management, possibly coupled with the deliberate reintroduction of the species to suitable sites.

Short-term fluctuations in populations are mainly due to weather conditions, particularly during the flight period. In cool, wet weather fewer eggs are laid and the mortality of young larvae is greater, thus there are fewer adults in the following year.

BLACK-VEINED WHITE, *Aporia crataegi*

Unfortunately, this extremely attractive butterfly became extinct as a breeding species in Britain in the 1920s. In the early nineteenth century black-veined whites bred in most counties south of Yorkshire, but a severe decline followed, though there were still periods of abundance in some localities. By 1900 it was reduced to a few populations in Kent, Worcestershire and Sussex. The largest colonies bred in Kent, but even there it became very rare after 1914 and the last confirmed record was at Herne Bay in 1922. The last British colony died out in Worcestershire in 1923. Since then only very occasional sightings of single specimens have been made, and these were almost certainly migrants from the continent or specimens bred from continental stock that escaped or were released.

As the name of the butterfly implies, the veins on its wings are black, contrasting strongly with the white interveinal areas (figure 28). The caterpillars feed on the leaves of hawthorn (*Crataegus*), blackthorn (*Prunus spinosa*) and fruit trees such as plum, damson and apple. During the winter they hibernate in a communal nest of silk and emerge in the spring to continue feeding. This species used to be a serious pest in orchards in parts of Europe but is now much scarcer. It is still found throughout central and southern Europe and occurs as far north as Scandinavia. The butterflies fly from May to June and are often found in clover and lucerne fields.

Various theories have been propounded to account for the demise of the black-veined white in Britain, but the cause is still a mystery. It is unlikely that changes in climate or habitat alone were the cause, and the decline occurred before the advent of effective insecticides. There may have been a coincidence of several factors, one of which was probably the incidence of several years with high September rainfall, which could have caused high larval mortality. It is also possible that there was an epidemic of a virus or fungal disease, or even increased predation by birds.

There have been several attempts to reintroduce this butterfly to the British Isles by releasing stock from Europe. It was tried at Sandwich in Kent in the 1930s, in Winston Churchill's garden at Westerham, Kent, in 1948-9 and in Surrey in the 1970s, but there was no long-term establishment. More knowledge of the precise ecological requirements of this butterfly is needed to give a basis for introduction and subsequent management.

BATH WHITE, *Pontia daplidice*

This butterfly is a very rare migrant to Britain, though occasionally, as in 1906

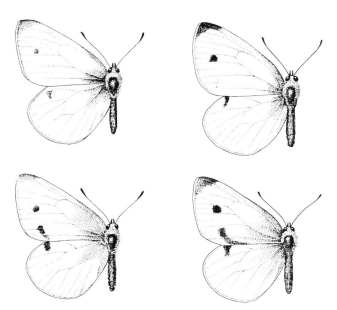

21. *Sex and brood differences in small white: (top left) spring-brood male; (top right) summer-brood male; (bottom left) spring-brood female; (bottom right) summer-brood female.*

22. *Sex and brood differences in large white: (top left) spring-brood male; (top right) summer-brood male; (bottom left) spring-brood female; (bottom right) summer-brood female.*

15

23. *Small white.*

24. *Large white. The dark area on the wing tip extends further down the outer margin of the wing than on the small white.*

25. *Underside of large white.*

26. *Large white (female).*

27. *Wood white.*

28. *Black-veined white.*

The yellows

29. *Chrysalises of wood white.*

BRIMSTONE, *Gonepteryx rhamni*
    This lovely butterfly is one of the first to emerge in spring and may be seen on warm, sunny days in April or even earlier. The males are the first to appear and they often visit sallow catkins or yellow flowers, such as dandelions and primroses, in order to find nectar and thereby replenish their energy reserves. Mating probably occurs soon after the females emerge; during courtship the butterflies engage in upward spiralling flights.
    The brimstone is quite a large butterfly, with a wingspan of around 60 mm. The males are a bright sulphur yellow, with the females a paler lemon with a greenish tint. Both sexes have an orange spot on each wing. When resting or feeding they always keep the wings closed so only the undersides are visible (figure 31). In this position they are superbly camouflaged, if amongst vegetation, as the outline of the wings is leaf-shaped (figure 30) and the veins on the wings are prominent, resembling those on a leaf. Brimstones overwinter in the adult stage and probably spend this time concealed amongst dense evergreen vegetation such as ivy or holly. This species is one of the longest-lived of British butterflies, some individuals living for eleven months.
    The foodplants of the brimstone are the common or purging buckthorn (*Rhamnus cartharticus*), which prefers chalky soils, and alder buckthorn (*Frangula alnus*), which occurs mainly on wetter or acidic soils. The distribution of the brimstone in Britain follows that of its foodplants very closely, thus it is fairly common throughout most of southern England as far north as Humberside but becomes less common further north. It is extremely rare in Scotland. It is very local in Wales, except in the south-west and near the south coast, and in Ireland is largely confined to areas of limestone soils. The range of the brimstone does not seem to have changed since records have been kept. Brimstones are often seen well away from their usual habitats, even straying into urban areas. This

and 1945, appreciable numbers arrive. In those years they bred on wild crucifers and colonies of some tens or hundreds of butterflies were temporarily established in a few south-coast localities. However, in most years only one or two Bath whites are recorded and in many years none are seen. Most sightings are in late summer, usually on southern cliffs or downs. The undersides of the wings are superficially similar to an orange-tip's, but paler. The dark markings on the upperside are different to other British whites: there is a black mark rather like a pawprint in the centre of the forewing and a series of black blotches at the tip. The female has dark marks on the hindwing.
    Bath whites are resident in southern Europe and North Africa but are strong migrants, regularly flying to other parts of Europe and occasionally reaching northern areas such as Britain.

18

tendency to fly in areas well removed from any buckthorns has led to speculation that brimstones may be able to breed on other plants, but although they have been observed to lay eggs on other species, successful breeding has not been recorded.

The off-white, bottle-shaped eggs are laid between mid April and early July, being deposited singly on buds, leaves and terminal shoots. There appears to be a preference for bushes 2 to 3 metres high in sunny positions. Even the most isolated bushes may be chosen, as female brimstones have an extraordinary ability to find the foodplant amongst other vegetation. The caterpillar hatches after about ten days. Initially it makes small feeding holes in the leaves but as it grows it will consume whole leaves. The caterpillars are bluish-green and are well camouflaged as they rest along the midrib of the leaf. They can be found between early May and August, taking about a month to complete their development. When fully fed they usually move away from the foodplant to pupate among low-growing vegetation.

The summer generation of adults emerge in August and from then until October or November, when they seek hibernation sites, they build up their food reserves by feeding on nectar from flowers. Their proboscis, the tube through which they suck up the nectar, is long (17 mm), enabling them to feed on flowers with long corollas, such as knapweeds and teasels. In late summer and autumn brimstones may be seen in groups at favoured sites along woodland edges or rides.

CLOUDED YELLOW, *Colias croceus*

Of the three species of clouded yellow that migrate to the British Isles, *C. croceus* is by far the most common, though even in the case of this species the numbers reaching Britain vary a great deal from year to year. In the winter the clouded yellow is mainly restricted to the Mediterranean region and there it may have up to four annual generations. Later in the year, as numbers increase, some migrate into northern Europe and breed there. In Britain the highest numbers occur in southern England and southern Ireland, the first landfalls for migrants from Europe. They then spread north in diminishing numbers, occasionally reaching Scotland. The first migrants usually arrive in May or June and, if these are reasonably numerous and breed successfully, there may be a much larger second generation in August and September. They have little chance of surviving the winter in Britain because no stage of the life cycle is adapted for hibernation.

Females lay their pale yellow eggs singly on the leaves of clovers, lucerne, trefoils and melilots, and can produce up to six hundred. The deep-green caterpillars have a covering of fine white hairs and a yellow or whitish stripe along each side. The chrysalis is pale yellow-green, and is well hidden.

The male clouded yellow is usually orange-yellow on the upperside, with broad black borders to the wings, which have a span of around 57 mm. There is a black spot near the centre of each forewing and a deep orange spot in the centre of each hindwing. The females are slightly larger and have yellow spots in the black borders. There is considerable variation in the ground colour of the uppersides: males vary from pale chrome-yellow to deep orange and females have a very pale yellowish-white form known as *C. croceus helice*. This form usually makes up 5 to 10 per cent of the population and is difficult to distinguish from the pale clouded and Berger's clouded yellows, particularly when in flight. The black border on the hindwing of *helice* is darker and broader and the border on the forewing extends further round the lower edge.

When clouded yellows settle they rarely open their wings, so usually only the undersides are visible. These are deep yellow with a black spot halfway across the forewing and a reddish-brown area containing a silver mark shaped like a figure-of-eight in the centre of the hindwing (figure 32). The head and body are also yellow.

PALE CLOUDED YELLOW, *Colias hyale*

This butterfly is a much rarer migrant to the British Isles than the clouded yellow and most records are from the

30. *Brimstone, show-ing its resemblance to a dead leaf.*

31. *Brimstone.*

32. *Clouded yellow.*

southern coastal regions of England. It does not get as far north as *C. croceus*. In Europe its range extends through central areas to southern Russia and it sometimes appears in large numbers on the North Sea coasts of Germany and the Netherlands. It is rare for more than three hundred individuals to be recorded in any one year in Britain and there are often far fewer than this. In 1900 over two thousand were seen, however, and there were over eight hundred in 1947, the 'clouded yellow year'. However, large numbers of this species do not invariably accompany large migrations of *C. croceus*; in 1983 only six definite observations of *C. hyale* were made, compared with over thirteen thousand *C. croceus*.

The first pale clouded yellows usually arrive in Britain in May or June and these may breed to produce more butterflies in August or September. The caterpillars are green with a broken red and orange line along each side. They feed on lucerne, clovers and vetches.

Pale clouded yellows have a lighter ground colour to the wings than most clouded yellows. Males are primrose yellow and females usually almost white. Both sexes have a broad black margin with spots of the ground colour within this border near the tip of the forewing. There is a black spot near the middle of the forewing and a pale orange spot on the hindwing. This butterfly is particularly attracted to fields of lucerne or clover. It is unable to survive the British winter.

BERGER'S CLOUDED YELLOW, *Colias australis*

This butterfly was not recognised as a separate species from the pale clouded yellow until 1947. It is now known to occur throughout central and southern Europe. It is much rarer in Britain than *C. hyale*, with only occasional sightings, usually near the south coast.

It has a brighter colour than *C. hyale*, the black border on the forewing is narrower and that on the hindwing is almost absent in *australis*. Also, the orange spot on the hindwing is much brighter in *australis*. The caterpillar of Berger's clouded yellow also looks different; it is green with yellow stripes and black spots. It feeds on different foodplants to *hyale*, choosing horse-shoe vetch (*Hippocrepis comosa*) and crown vetch (*Coronilla varia*). This butterfly is most often seen on rough chalky ground and hillsides, habitats where these foodplants occur.

Studying Pierids

OBSERVING PIERIDS

Large and small whites are very common in gardens, where they can be seen feeding on many different flowers. They are particularly fond of lavender, catmint and buddleia. In the countryside they can often be seen on composites such as dandelions, knapweeds and scabious. The green-veined white also likes to feed from composites, including ragwort, but also feeds on many other flowers such as bugle and stitchwort. Both small and green-veined whites may sometimes be seen, often in groups, drinking from puddles or wet mud, especially in hot weather.

Orange-tip butterflies feed on a variety of flowers such as garlic and hedge mustards, lady's smock, bugle, charlock, bluebells, stitchwort and vetches. In areas where they are fairly abundant they may fly into gardens and there they may use honesty, sweet rocket and dame's violet both as sources of nectar and also as foodplants for their caterpillars. If these plants are grown, breeding colonies may be established and these beautiful butterflies encouraged to stay in the garden. Alternatively, a place can be found in the garden for their wild foodplants, garlic mustard (Jack by the hedge) or lady's smock (cuckoo flower). Lady's smock can look very attractive in a wet part of the garden. Seeds of these wild plants can be collected from the countryside or purchased from wild flower seedsmen. It has to be remembered that the seeds and flowers of endangered species may not be picked or the plants dug up anywhere. Plants may not be dug up on land belonging to someone else.

Hedgerows, the edges of woods and wet areas near rivers are the best places for observing green-veined whites and orange-tips. In sunny weather in spring females can be seen searching for food-plants on which to lay eggs and males can be observed searching for mates or de-fending territories. When orange-tips stop flying and rest on vegetation with wings closed they become very difficult to spot, particularly when on a flowerhead of hedge parsley, which is matched very closely by the green mottled pattern of their undersides.

Brimstones will sometimes fly into gardens, but are more often seen around woods. Their flower preferences seem to change with the time of year. In the spring they feed mainly on yellow flowers such as primroses, dandelions and sal-lows, whereas the second brood prefer purple flowers such as knapweeds, this-tles, teasel, dead-nettles, marjoram, be-tony and wild basil. Brimstones flying in the autumn may visit ivy blossom. In gardens they have been observed feeding on buddleia and scarlet geraniums. In areas where female brimstones occur it would be worth planting a buckthorn bush in the garden in the hope of induc-ing egg-laying.

When large immigrations of clouded yellows occur they can often be seen in numbers in fields of lucerne or clover, though they will also visit other flowers including ragwort, dandelion and hawk-weeds.

BREEDING PIERIDS

Most Pierids are fairly easy to breed, the best example being the large white, which is cultured by many universities, colleges and schools to provide material for educational purposes or scientific research. The large white has been inten-sively studied by scientists in many parts of the world and much information gained on its physiology and biochemis-try. This work is summarised in Feltwell (1982).

Even with species that are easy to rear, however, great care has to be taken to prevent the spread of virus and other diseases and a sharp lookout has to be kept for parasitoids. A detailed account of breeding methods and of cages and other equipment needed can be found in Cribb (1983) and Friedrich (1986).

It is important to rear larvae of the orange-tip separately because of their cannibalistic tendencies. One convenient method of doing this is to place flower-heads of one of their foodplants, each with one larva, in pieces of wet florist's Oasis. Seed pods of honesty and horse-radish are possible alternatives to garlic mustard and lady's smock. Each larva needs at least four seed pods to complete its development. When fully grown they will wander from the foodplant so need to be confined at this stage in a cage with stems provided for pupation sites. Green-veined whites can also be reared on honesty and horseradish, with arabis pro-viding another alternative to wild cruci-fers. This species feeds on leaves rather than seed pods.

The best way of rearing some species is to confine the larvae in a sleeve of black nylon mesh on a growing foodplant out-side. Brimstone caterpillars can be reared to the pupal stage in this way on buck-thorn and black-veined whites on haw-thorn or *Prunus* species. The sleeves protect them from predators such as birds, earwigs and spiders.

Many butterflies need a supply of both nectar and moisture if they are to survive in captivity and breed successfully. Water can be provided by spraying a fine mist over plants and the inside of cages at regular intervals, or by providing pieces of wet Oasis in a shallow tray. Pupae also need to be sprayed with water from time to time.

Wood whites require food and water and also shady areas in the cage. Flowers of chives have been used successfully as a source of nectar for this species and the larvae can be bred on bird's-foot trefoil. Most Pierids can be overwintered outside or in a cold outbuilding but clouded yellows have no hibernation stage and have to be provided with heat, light and suitable food through the winter.

Unless a thriving colony of one of the commoner species is found, stock should not be removed from the wild. Livestock, cages and other equipment can be obtained from specialised entomological dealers whose addresses can be found in the *Bulletin* of the Amateur Entomologists' Society (see Organisations).

Butterflies that have been bred in captivity should only be released into the countryside in consultation with the butterfly recorder for that county (often based at the county museum), the county naturalists' trust or the Nature Conservancy Council. Such releases could lead to false records and may be inappropriate on some sites for genetic or other reasons.

CONSERVATION

Of the Pierids that are still resident in the British Isles, the wood white is the species most in danger of extinction. However, the decline does seem to have been arrested and possibly even reversed. With the improved knowledge of its ecological requirements gained from the research by scientists at the Institute of Terrestrial Ecology, management plans can be formulated for sites where it occurs. Reintroductions into previously occupied sites can also be considered in conjunction with suitable management of these areas. It is important that as many as possible of these sites are acquired by conservation organisations so that the habitat can be protected and improved.

Orange-tips and green-veined whites are still common in many areas. However, even these species experience local extinctions. These may be due to removal of habitat by agricultural, industrial or housing development or the use by farmers or local authorities of herbicides which destroy the foodplants. Certainly, much of the spraying and mowing of roadside verges by some councils seems unnecessary and causes the loss of many foodplants and nectar sources.

Scientists working for the Game Conservancy are trying to convince arable farmers of the benefits of leaving the edges and headlands of fields unsprayed by insecticides and herbicides. This allows the survival of predators and parasites of cereal pests in these areas and also preserves the insects that provide food for partridge chicks. However, an additional benefit is the increase in the number of butterflies around such fields. Orange-tips and green-veined whites are two of the species that would benefit from this policy as it allows the survival of the wild crucifers on which they depend and reduces the chances of their caterpillars being killed by insecticide drift. Sowing wild flower seed mixtures containing appropriate crucifers could also provide new food sources in suitable habitats.

MONITORING BUTTERFLY DISTRIBUTION

There is a national monitoring scheme for British butterflies organised by the British Butterfly Conservation Society (see Organisations) in conjunction with the Biological Records Centre. Many counties have their own recording schemes and several county atlases of butterfly distribution have been published. Details should be available from county natural history museums or naturalists' trusts. These organisations welcome records and the results help to establish the current status of threatened species so that appropriate conservation measures can be undertaken.

Useful information

FURTHER READING

Carter, D. *Butterflies and Moths in Britain and Europe*. Pan, 1982.

Courtney, S. P. 'The Ecology of Pierid Butterflies: Dynamics and Interactions', *Advances in Ecological Research*, 15 (1986), pages 51-131.

Cribb, P. W. *Breeding the British Butterflies*. Amateur Entomologists' Society, 1983.

Emmet, A. Maitland, and Sokoloff, Paul A. (editors). *The Moths and Butterflies of Great Britain and Ireland*, Volume 7 (Part 1) 'The Hesperiidae to Nymphalidae (The Butterflies)'. Harley, 1989.

Feltwell, J. *The Large White Butterfly*. Dr W. Junk, 1982.

Feltwell, J. *The Natural History of Butterflies*. Croom Helm, 1986.

Friedrich, E. *Breeding Butterflies and Moths*. Harley, 1986.

Heath, J.; Pollard, E.; and Thomas, J. A. *Atlas of Butterflies in Britain and Ireland*. Viking, 1984.

Howarth, T. G. *South's British Butterflies*. Warne, 1973.

Newman, L. H. *Create a Butterfly Garden*. John Baker, 1967.

Thomas, J. A. *RSNC Guide to Butterflies of the British Isles*. Country Life/Newnes, 1986.

Whalley, P. *Butterfly Watching*. Severn House, 1980.

JOURNALS

Entomologist's Gazette, E. W. Classey Limited, PO Box 93, Park Road, Faringdon, Oxfordshire SN7 7DR.

Entomologist's Record, 31 Oakdene Road, Brockham, Betchworth, Surrey RH3 7JU.

ORGANISATIONS

Conservation societies

The British Butterfly Conservation Society, Tudor House, 102 Chaveney Road, Quorn, Loughborough, Leicestershire LE12 9AD. Telephone: 0509 412870.

The National Trust, PO Box 30, Beckenham, Kent BR3 4TL. Telephone: 01-464 1111.

The Nature Conservancy Council, Northminster House, Peterborough PE1 1UA. Telephone: 0733 40345.

The Royal Society for Nature Conservation, 22 The Green, Nettleham, Lincoln LN2 2NR. Telephone: 0522 752326. Co-ordinates county naturalists' trusts.

The Woodland Trust, Autumn Park, Dysart Road, Grantham, Lincolnshire NG31 6LL. Telephone: 0476 74297.

The World Wildlife Fund UK, Panda House, 11-13 Ockford Road, Godalming, Surrey GU7 1QU. Telephone: 04868 20551.

Other societies

Amateur Entomologists' Society, 355 Hounslow Road, Hanworth, Feltham, Middlesex TW13 5JH.

British Entomological and Natural History Society, c/o The Alpine Club, 74 South Audley Street, London WIY 5FF. Telephone: 01-499 1542.

ACKNOWLEDGEMENTS

Illustrations are acknowledged as follows: David Chambers, cover, 8, 25, 26; Vernon Hucks, 29, 32; Chris Rose, 2, 4, 21, 22; Mike Scutt, 3, 6. All others are by the author.